W9-BLK-349

DEAD

CHILDREN PLAYING

DEAD
CHILDREN
PLAYING

A Picture Book

stanley donwood & dr. tchock

This edition first published by Verso 2007

Previous edition published by IguapopGallery 2006

1 3 5 7 9 10 8 6 4 2

Verso
UK: 6 Meard Street, London W1F 0EG
USA: 180 Varick Street, New York, NY 10014-4606
www.versobooks.com

Verso is the imprint of New Left Books

ISBN-13: 978-1-84467-170-0

British Library Cataloguing in Publication Data
A catalogue record for this book is available from the British Library

Library of Congress Cataloging-in-Publication Data
A catalog record for this book is available from the Library of Congress

Printed and bound in Singapore by Tien Wah Press

low to use
our inhaler
properly

Remove the cover from the mouthpiece and shake the inhaler vigorously.

Holding the inhaler as shown, breathe out gently (but not fully) and then immediately . . .

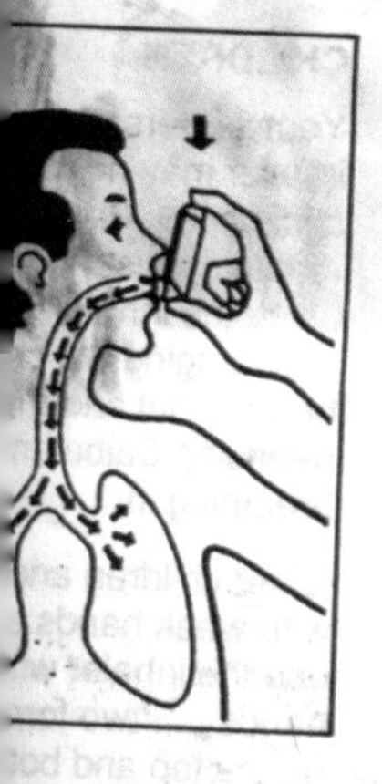

mouthpiece in the
l close your lips
After starting to
slowly and
ough your mouth,
nhaler firmly, as
elease
l and continue to

5
ONE . . . TWO . . .
THREE . . . FOUR . . . FIVE
. . . SIX . . . SEVEN . . . EIGHT
. . . NINE . . . TEN

Hold your breath for 10 seconds, or as long as is comfortable, before breathing out slowly.

6

If you are to take a second inhalation you should wait at least one minute before repeating steps 2, 3 and 4.

7

After use replace the cover on the mouthpiece.

Chemists

KEEP OUT OF CHILDREN'S REACH

SALBUTAMOL INHALER 10P

To be used as directed by your doctor

MR 10D

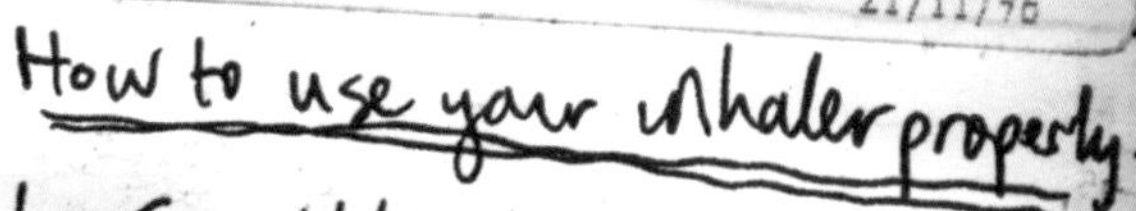

How to use your inhaler properly.

1. Scrabble around on the floor trying to find it.
2. Desperately fling away the cover from the mouthpiece and place the mouthpiece in the mouth.
3. Press the inhaler firmly, with increasing agitation, about five times.
4. Try to hold your breath, gasping in the Salbutamol.
5. Realise with terror that it isn't working.
6. Try very hard not to panic. Seek

... stimulants (sympathomimetics)

SALBUTAMOL (Ventolin etc) is a SELECTIVE BETA$_2$ ADRENOCEPTOR STIMULANT.

side effects: fine tremor (usually hands), nervous tension, headache, peripheral vasodilation, tachycardia (seldom troublesome when given by aerosol inhalation) hypokalaemia after high doses, hypersensitivity reactions including paradoxical bronchospasm, uticaria, and angioedema reported; slight pain on intramuscular injection

COX

Contains: 100 micrograms Salbutamol BP per actuation

Read the instruction leaflet before use

POM PL 0530/0246

COX

Salbutamol
INHALER

Salbutamol Aerosol Inhalation BP

200 metered actuations

COX PHARMACEUTICALS

COX

It is dangerous to exceed the recommended dose

Pressurised can: Do not puncture break or burn even when empty

Avoid storage in direct sunlight or heat
Store in a cool place
Protect from frost

KEEP ALL MEDICINES AWAY FROM CHILDREN

A H Cox & Co Ltd
Whiddon Valley
Barnstaple
England UK

~~OXYGEN~~ OXYGEN

Oxygen should be regarded as a drug.

It is prescribed for hypoxaemic patients to increase alveolar oxygen tension and decrease the work of breathing necessary to maintain a given arterial oxygen tension. The concentration depends on the condition

HAUNTED ATTIC:

NE PORVIVAĴO NUR
MORTIGI TEMPO*

MORTIGI TEMPO

Computer art
It is not always that one wants to design a use
product: artists are using computer graphics w
hundreds of colours to create exciting pictures
capable of moving and changing, rather like a
sophisticated cartoon. Some have developed
robots which draw pictures which have been
accepted and sold by art galleries.

Whenever a computer is switched on it waits to
told what to do. Computers are not independen
machines with brains. They are without any
intelligence as we recognise it in human beings.

Some organisations collect data about people
without their knowing that the data will be kept,
to what use it will be put. They watch people
constantly, using the data when they need it.

Fewer jobs?
While it is true that computers can work very fa
and remove the drudgery from boring tasks, ma
people are frightened that they will lose their jo
Robots have taken over in car factories where
engineers used to assemble parts. Word

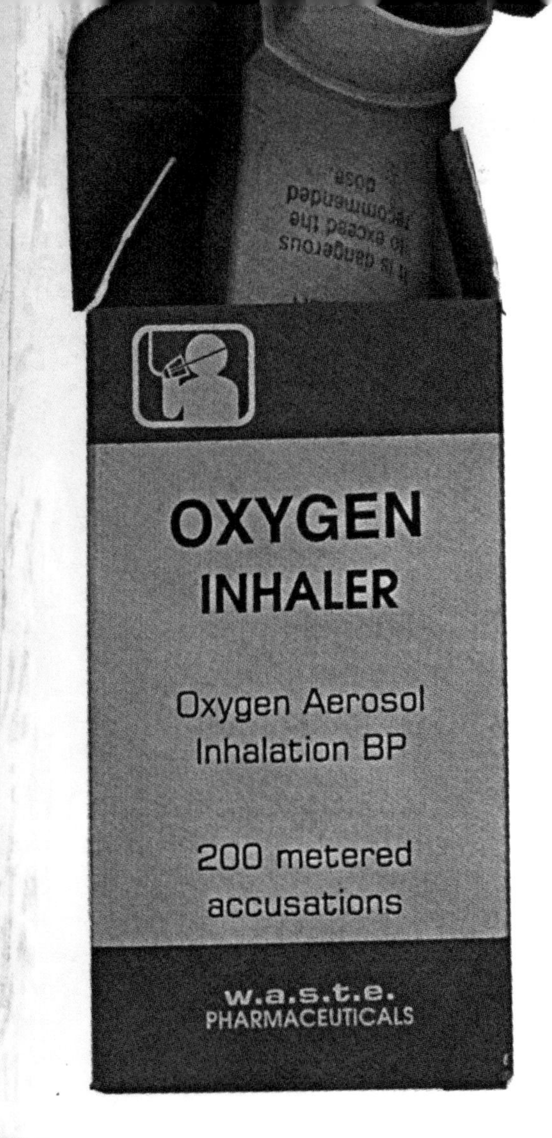

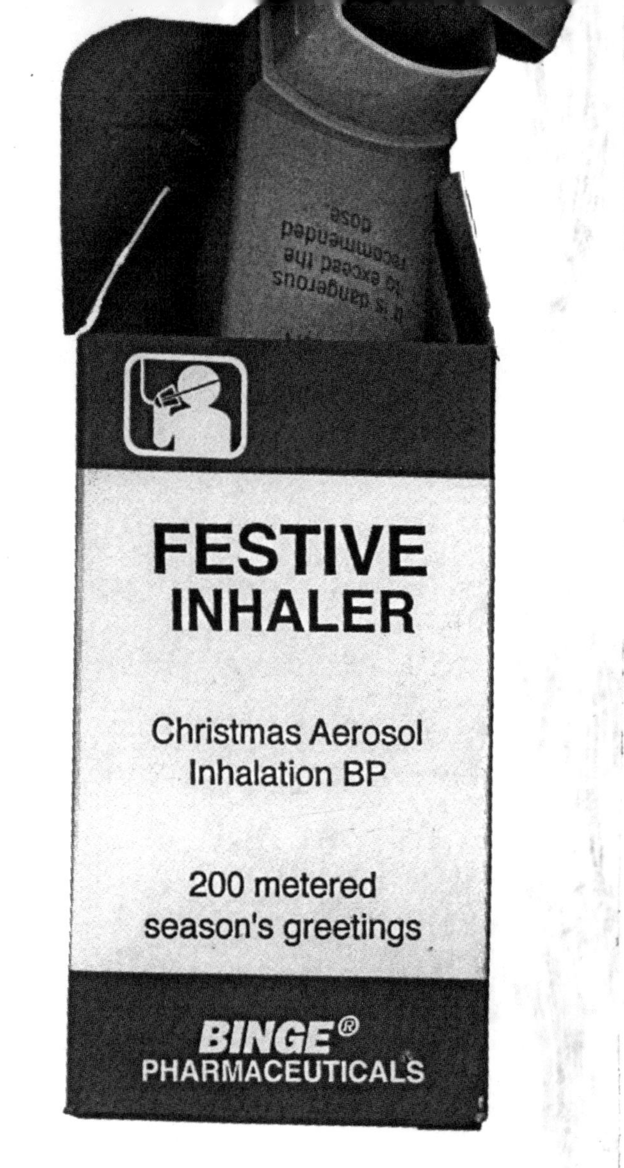

LIFE IS A BOWL OF FUCKING CHERRIE

AN
OTHERWISE
HEALTHY
INDIVIDUAL.

IT'S A PITY SHE FORGOT.
IT SEEMS I WAS WRONG.
IT'S A PITY SHE FORGOT.
IT SEEMS I WAS WRONG

I'm in a staggeringly cold studio that I've rented, and the rain is lashing at the large window that I can't manage to properly close. The view is of a line of sewerage pipe-cleaning lorries. The news is dominated by the concurrent wars in Kosovo. The Racak 'incident' has recently taken place. I'm a pampered UK citizen, but I recognise the logos on the clothes of those pulled from rubble, I recognise the types of trees around the burning villages, and guiltily I realise that this conflict is affecting me like none has before. This feels as if, with a little bad luck, it could be me in the news. My girlfriend. My kids.

I'm sitting at the bar in the pub, reading a newspaper. On the front is a photograph. It's taken looking straight down at the ground, and the image is of perhaps a square metre of snow. The snow is spattered with blood, engine oil, marked with bootprints, studded with cigarette ends. Snow. Snow is a gentle blanket that makes our ugly world beautiful, a gleaming raiment that conceals the tawdriness of litter, *shit and trash. But not here.* Snow is evidence.

I've got a memory, long forgotten, that's just resurfaced. When I was a boy, on one of my extremely infrequent visits to the capital from the badlands of Essex, *I saw some paintings, paintings on a monumental scale of what would now be called atrocities; redcoated English soldiers massacring foreigners. To my young eyes these depictions of long-ago battles looked like jewellery scattered in mud, beautiful tableaux of gems of colour arranged in dun brown fields. I resolve to see these paintings once more. I need to see them. That's what I want to paint; jewels strewn in snow. Somehow I want to MAKE THE HORRIBLE BEAUTIFUL...*

So I'm in London, and I'm looking for the pictures. I try the obvious places, the National Gallery, *the* Tate: *nothing. I try further afield at the* Imperial War Museum, *the* National Army Museum, *a few less-*

well-known galleries: nothing. I ask around, but no-one seems to know what I'm on about. But realistically these paintings must exist; they're the record of the British Empire, they're the heroic record of 'our' valiant redcoats. But where are they? I guess that between the Seventies, when I remember seeing these pictures, and the late Nineties, which is now, they've been hidden away in archives. I could probably request to see them, but I'm handicapped by not knowing what they're called or who they're by. And I'm losing the energy to find them. This search has taken me a fruitless week.

ANOTHER MEMORY; a comic by Alan Moore and Bill Sienkiewicz called 'Shadowplay: The Secret Team', in which the number of the dead were tallied by images of red swimming pools. The average human body holds a gallon of blood. The average swimming pool holds 50,000 gallons of water. The maths, and the graphic, were inescapable.

These are hard paintings to make. They are ostensibly for a record that is proving a hard record to make. No-one knows what it's going to be called, but later on it gets to be called 'Kid A'.

Red snow. Bootprints. (1999) 168cm x 168cm. Acrylic on canvas.

Residential nemesis. (1999) 168cm x 168cm. Acrylic and charcoal on canvas.

Get out before Saturday. (2000) 168cm x 168cm. Acrylic on canvas.

Avert your eyes. (2000) 168cm x 168cm. Acrylic, charcoal and paper on canvas.

Trade center. (2000) 168cm x 168cm. Acrylic, charcoal and blackboard paint on canvas.

Hotels and a swimming pool. (2000) 168cm x 168cm. Acrylic, charcoal and gravel on canvas.

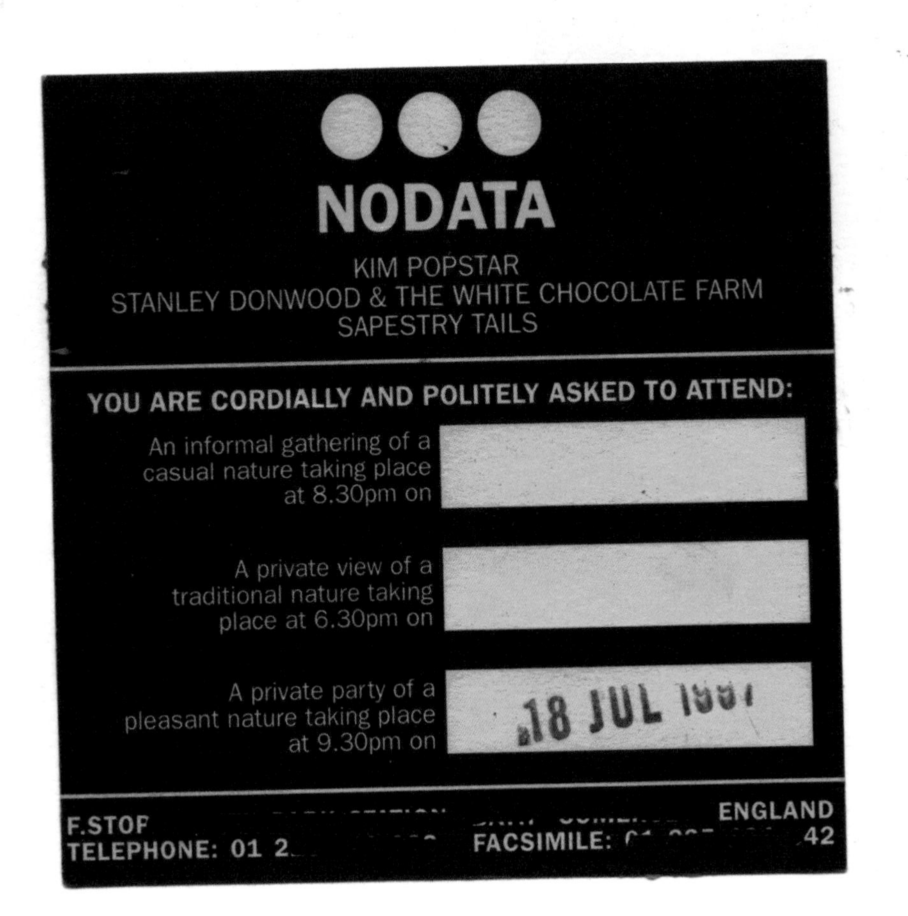

NODATA
KIM POPSTAR
STANLEY DONWOOD & THE WHITE CHOCOLATE FARM
SAPESTRY TAILS
YOU ARE CORDIALLY AND POLITELY ASKED TO ATTEND:
An informal gathering of a casual nature taking place at 8.30pm on
A private view of a traditional nature taking place at 6.30pm on
A private party of a pleasant nature taking place at 9.30pm on
18 JUL 1997
F.STOP
ENGLAND
TELEPHONE: 01 2
FACSIMILE:
42

GIVE UP.

Love Story.

I am driving a fast car along the beautiful cliffs t
line the road from London to Brighton. To my lef
gleams the azure Mediterranean. The car is a
of control as the brakes have been sabotag
[illegible] the cliffs flash past unti

LOST

INTEGRITY

IF FOUND

PLEASE RETURN TO

ON AIR

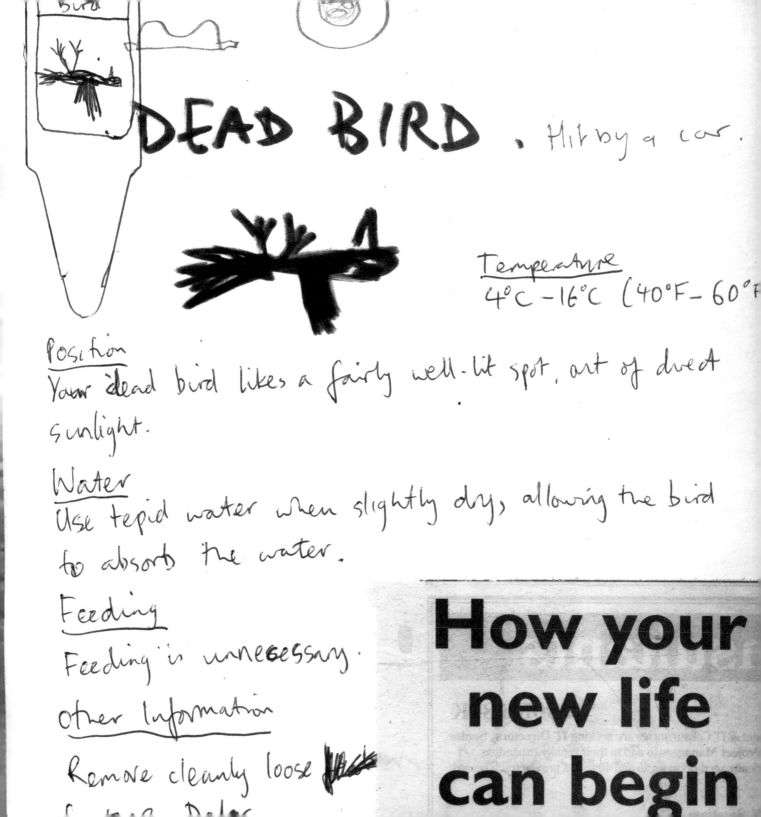

DEAD BIRD

. Hit by a car.

Temperature
4°C – 16°C (40°F – 60°F

Position
Your dead bird likes a fairly well-lit spot, out of direct sunlight.

Water
Use tepid water when slightly dry, allowing the bird to absorb the water.

Feeding
Feeding is unnecessary.

Other Information
Remove cleanly loose 

How your new life can begin

Lost Child,
against demons
Lost Child

Lost Child,
Lost Child,
Child

Lost Child,
Lost Child,
against
against demons
Lost Child

Lost Child,

War village. (2000) 168cm x 84cm. Acrylic and charcoal on canvas.

First Minos wall. (2000) 168cm x 168cm. Acrylic, charcoal and spray paint on canvas.

I'm in London, and I'm not sure what I'm doing. I've got a video camera and I'm filming nothing in particular, as is proved when I stop for a cup of coffee and look at the footage I've shot so far. It's just buildings, streets, people. It's exactly what I've seen.

The trouble is that what I think I'm seeing bears little relation to what I'm actually seeing. Fascinated by a brief mention of Piranesi in Peter Ackroyd's 'The House of Doctor Dee', I boarded the train to London seeking an imaginary prison, a labyrinth of half-hidden treasures, *thronged with mysteries and illuminated by an invisible lace of past events. I've got my worn copy of the* **A-Z** *and a guidebook to London published in* 1911, *a notebook filled with mostly monosyllabic words transcribed (with some difficulty) from the tags that decorate the city, and I've got this fucking video camera.*

The camera is the problem, and it takes me a day to realise it. It's not reality that I'm looking for. It goes back in my bag, and I stand at the edge of Ludgate Circus, *staring at the vehicles dancing on the squashed yellow diamonds painted on the wet tarmac.*

Since I started drawing little weeping minotaurs I've been trying to find the maze. Hours of study and several journeys to famous mazes have ultimately led me here; to London. London is the labyrinth, the miz-maze, the original troy town. My 1911 *guidebook takes me all over the city, seeking markers and signifiers. I'm briefly elated to find the London Stone, embedded not in a church any longer, but in the wall of a shop selling trainers. A tourist bus glides past, a phalanx of cameras recording my confusion at being surprised on my knees on the pavement, apparently worshipping the foundations of the sports shop. This isn't the last time that my secret discoveries turn out to be items on the tourist itinerary. London has been* mapped exhaustively *and documented many times before.*

I'm trying to make work that will describe the Radiohead record that will eventually be called 'Amnesiac'. The figure of the weeping minotaur, a cursed monster condemned to live and die *in a* subterranean labyrinth, *is my guide. I want to make the walls of the maze, to daub and scratch the frustrations of the monster in the cage. My plotless, aimless perambulations in the city are decided by subconscious decisions; LEFT, LEFT, straight ahead, RIGHT...*

Everywhere now I'm finding traces of the minotaur's path, from Smithfield, *where the bulls were herded from* Bartholomew's Fair, *along* Giltspur Street, *past the* Old Bailey, *down* Fleet Street, *up* Cornhill.. *The tags of graffiti writers echo in my head as I stare out at the* Thames *from* Cousin Lane.

And I've overdone it all, as usual. I've read a lot of what's been written about London, from the history of economic systems that support the wealthy to the rumours of man-eating pigs roaming the sewers. But this time I've tried to stay out of the culture warehouses, the museums and galleries. The difficulty of working in the way I tend to is that the various fictions and theories I absorb solidify into a sort of cognitive concrete inside my skull, and after a while I can't distinguish fact from invention. They sacrifice children to stop the bridges from falling down. St Paul's stands on an ancient Druidic site. There are Underground stations far below the ones we know to service a subterranean train system in the event of nuclear war.

All I want to do is make representations of the walls that imprisoned the minotaur, the child of Queen Pasiphaë and the white bull, gift of Poseidon. Also a film. I'm going to make a film of a man running through London, possessed by the spirit of the minotaur, chased by his own imagination from Smithfield to the waves lapping the tiny shore at Cousin Lane...

What I don't know now is that this film will be made (one freezing winter day in the City), that I and the hastily assembled crew will almost be arrested by the City of London's private police force (having been surveilled by CCTV since we began filming) and that the film will later be utterly lost, never to resurface. The paintings also get made, and despite a quirky existence (transported by rickshaw; exhibited briefly in a derelict warehouse; stored for a few years in a corner of a factory in a remote industrial estate) are eventually, via a brief stay in my haunted dancehall of a studio, displayed in this book and in Spain, a country well known for bullfighting.

Second Minos wall. (2000) 168cm x 168cm. Acrylic, charcoal and spray paint on canvas.

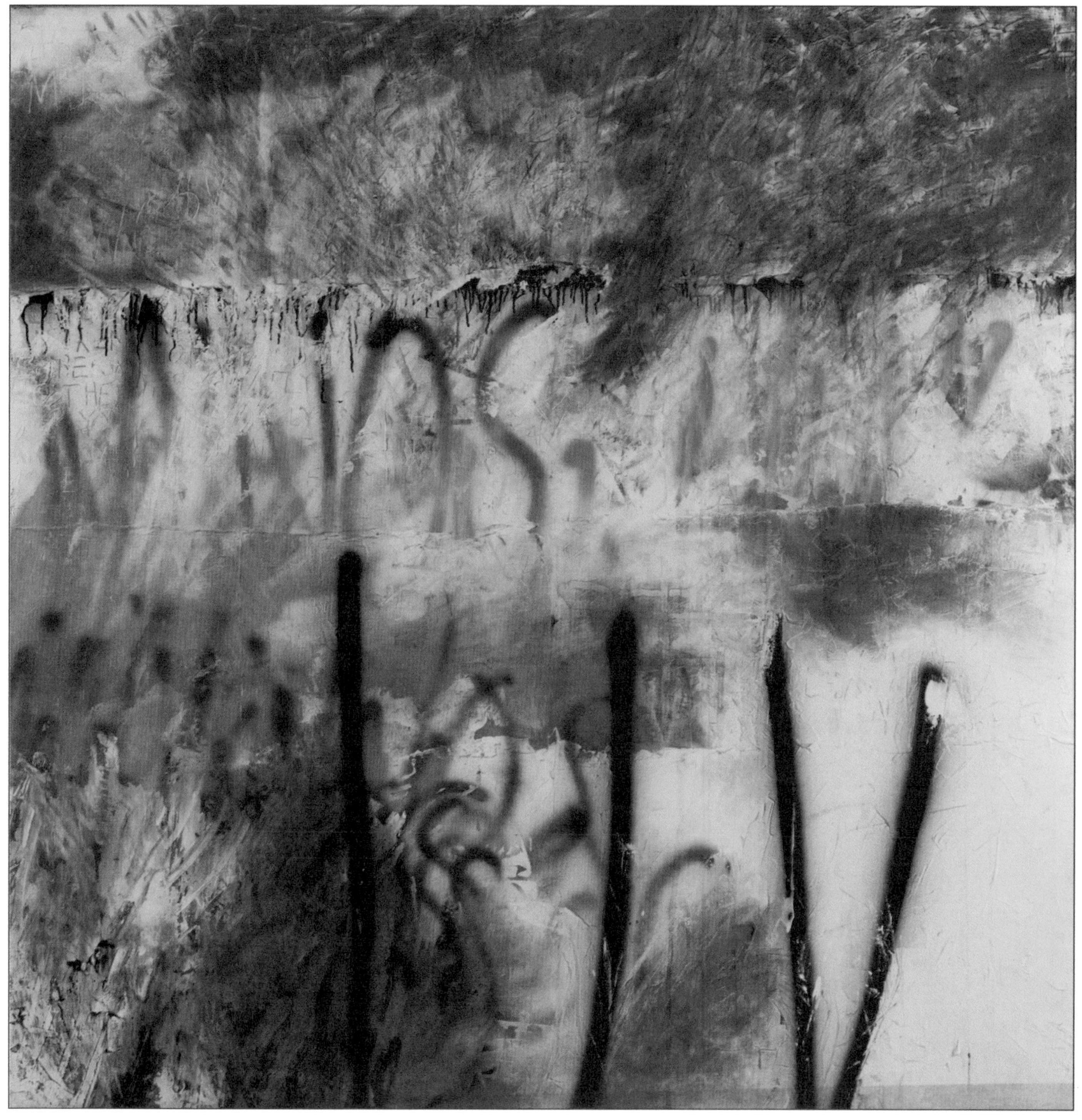

Third Minos wall. (2000) 168cm x 168cm. Acrylic, charcoal and spray paint on canvas.

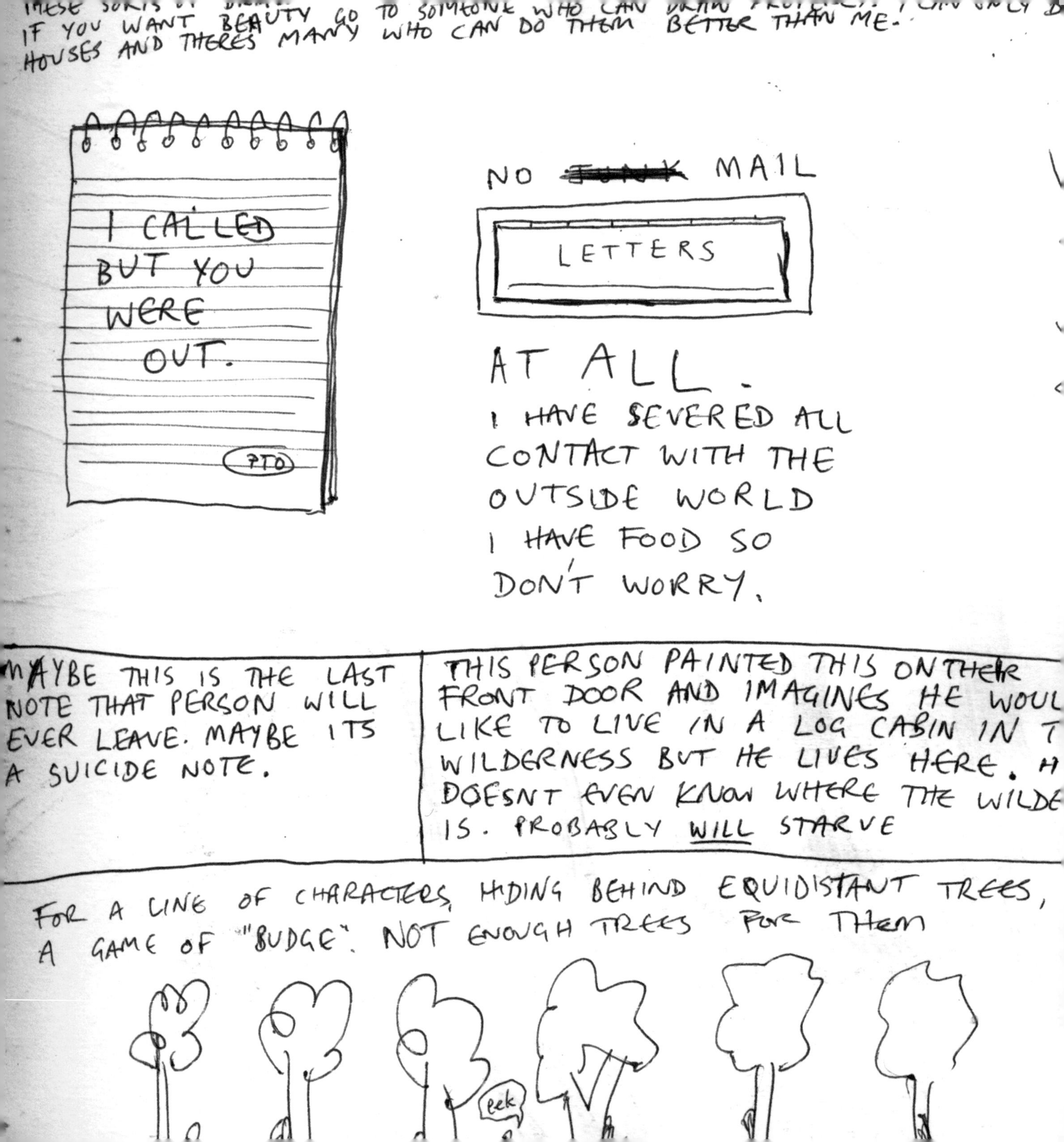
IF YOU WANT BEAUTY GO TO SOMEONE WHO CAN DRAW PROPERLY. I CAN ONLY D
HOUSES AND THERES MANY WHO CAN DO THEM BETTER THAN ME.
I CALLED BUT YOU WERE OUT.
PTO
NO MAIL
LETTERS
AT ALL.
I HAVE SEVERED ALL CONTACT WITH THE OUTSIDE WORLD
I HAVE FOOD SO DON'T WORRY.
MAYBE THIS IS THE LAST NOTE THAT PERSON WILL EVER LEAVE. MAYBE ITS A SUICIDE NOTE.
THIS PERSON PAINTED THIS ON THEIR FRONT DOOR AND IMAGINES HE WOUL LIKE TO LIVE IN A LOG CABIN IN T WILDERNESS BUT HE LIVES HERE. H DOESNT EVEN KNOW WHERE THE WILDE IS. PROBABLY WILL STARVE
FOR A LINE OF CHARACTERS, HIDING BEHIND EQUIDISTANT TREES, A GAME OF "BUDGE". NOT ENOUGH TREES FOR THEM
eek

I'm NOT SCARED.

[illegible] Meacher, the Environment Minister, and Sir Kenneth Calman, the Chief Medical Officer, said: "This report clearly confirms that air pollution damages health."

The findings triggered immediate demands for a cut in road traffic. The British Medical Association warned: "The grim reaper comes early on days of heavy air pollution." Friends of the Earth said the deaths figure was "extremely alarming" and the British Lung Foundation described it as "very serious".

[illegible] the contribution of air pollution to their ill health tips the balance."

He said they were not necessarily extra deaths or hospital admissions but ones that had been "brought forward", in some cases by a few days, but in other cases by a "somewhat longer period". He compared the effect with that of the cold in winter, which is linked with 30,000 extra deaths.

Mr Meacher said the findings contained a "major lesson" for transport. A

fuel, are [illegible]

Professor Jon Ayres, a committee member, said it was likely that pollution had long-term effects on health but these remained to be proved. "What we would like to know is if you live in a town like London all your life, is it significantly shortened compared with living in a rural area. That is the big question."

— *Jeremy Laurance*

inserted in the interests of Security and Confidentiality

Carefully cut out these pieces and then paste
them in position on the black and white
page. In this way you can make a pretty
picture. Use the covers as guides to help
you complete your pictures.

Beautiful Story About

Theres just the muffled crunchy sound of teeth grinding and scraping of boots on
tarmac or something and a noise far away that maybe is someone crying or a cat
and everything moves a bit in the wind but there isnt any noise of that sort of
thing. Theres a tape on of people talking about probably nothing important at a
restaurant and a marching sound thats a bit like a lot of soldiers and a bit like a
wheel rubbing against metal but it might not be a tape its hard to tell. And
evryones run out of jokes because noones laughing at anything although they probl
would if they had a sense of humour. Probably nothing important. Just a noise in
the dark when youre halfasleep something behind the curtains dont look its nothir
dont look honestly its nothing. Maybe its the town you live in making these noise
or maybe its you. Just a million mobiles and modems squawking and spluttering
and hissing like piss on a fire like a million gallons of piss on an inferno just thi
[illegible] of that. Vertebrae being sawn apart sounds like this.

NOTHING NOTHING YOU JUST IMAGINED IT
A NOISE NOTHING A SILENCE JUST THE
HOUSE "SETTLING". WHOS THAT WHOS
THAT NOTHING IMAGINED IT WHOS THAT
OUT THERE/ IN THE KITCHEN THERES
NOTHING IN THE COLD COLD LIGHT
NOBODY BEHIND THE DOOR NOTHING
S THERE? DEAD PEOPLE' LIVE PEOPLE' ONE PERSON' NOTHING BEHIND YOU
INTO DUST
DOORS THAT OPEN AND SHUT
DOORS THAT OPEN AND SHUT
DOORS THAT OPEN AND SHUT
DOORS THAT OPEN AND SHUT
DOORS THAT OPEN AND SHUT

I WANT TO SEE YOU SMILE AGAIN
THE DAY THE BANKS COLLAPSE
ZEE HORDES OF VIGILANTEES
THE DAY THE BANKS COLLAPSE
ON US

I HAVE A PAPER HERE THAT ENTITLES ME TO FAST TRACK STATUS

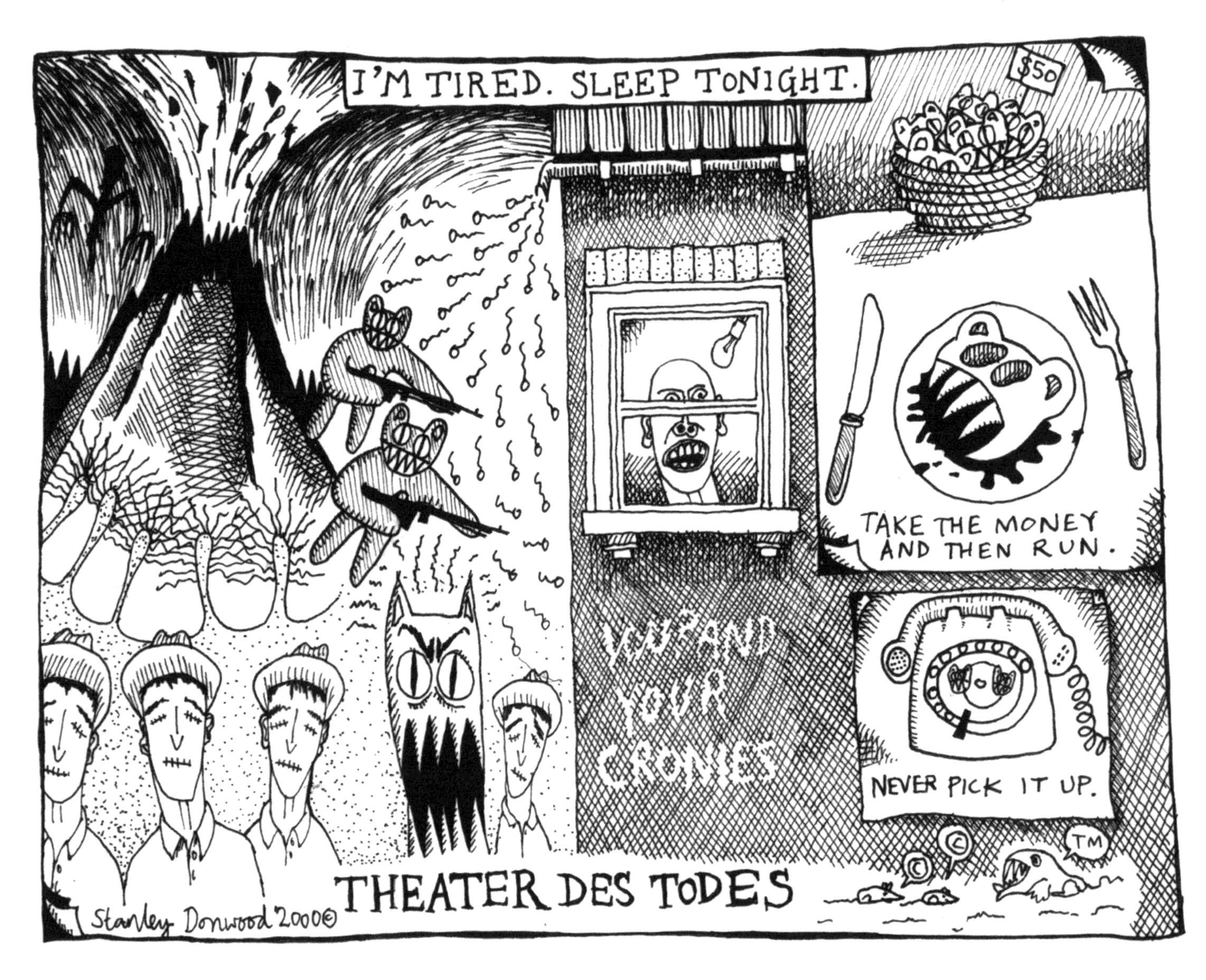

EVRYBODY STOPS AND GAWPS
EYES POPPED OUT LIKE CIGARETTE MACHINES

**RIGHT HAND PULL TRIGGER
LEFT HAND SHRUG SHOULDER**

FUCKIN MOUTH
ALL TOGETHER NOW:
AND THE WIND WONT BLOW
AND I WONT KNOW
BECAUSE I WILL BE DEAD
DEAD DEAD DEAD DEAD
DEAD DEAD DEAD DEAD
DEAD DEAD DEAD DEAD
DEAD DEAD.
DESPOT©
HES A
MARVELLOUS
BARITONE

VICTOR & VANQUISHED : COMEDY DOUBLE
THATS ANOTHE
FINE MESS
YOUVE GOTTE
ME INTO

...ltwater. Brunkins composed of bodies. You are not alone.
...u are observed. Gentle needles you can hardly feel.
...ese woods and hills are the trademark of Woods
...nd Hills PLC. Countryside developments. This stylised
...andscape is private intellectual property. Never lost,
...lways observed. Filthy glaciers floating in detritus-strewn
...onic waters. With all this gone, everything I write is
...n fucked approximation of my own furious, misplaced and
...accurate? nostalgia. The past never happened except
...n books. I have made these monsters. I carved these
...glaciers from my frozen sperm. I coughed these icebergs
...his ditchwater, running fast past the carcasses
...of the unfortunate is what I pour down the
...ink - an alchemical bilge of opportunity, makeup, tears
...nd vomit. It's not real. I can only touch these flooded
...waters, lick the submerged grasses, kick my heels in the
...silt. Catch me while you can, because I'm gone from here

...umps become wet swellings. Wet swellings become poisoned
...weepings. Poisoned weepings become normal. All that's left
...are scars, scabs, and wounds that won't heal.

...regret to inform you that, according to official criteria, you

It's late summer, and I'm in the American city of Los Angeles,*getting around in other people's cars, taxis and buses. It's not really a city that encourages walking. The cliché is that walking can get you arrested, but in my limited experience walking is more likely to get you hot, bored and tired. So most of the time I'm in other people's cars, looking out of the window at a city scaled for private motor vehicles. I've got a bit of a problem with private motor vehicles, but in a place like this it's probably a good idea to KEEP MY MOUTH SHUT.*

Part of the massive scale of this particular version of hell on Earth involves the many advertising materials employed along the multilane highways that dissect this place. Designed and constructed with the assumption that they will be viewed from fast-moving vehicles by people who are assailed from all sides by a visual cacophony of conflicting messages, these advertising materials are big. Very Big, and Very Brash. *I quite like advertising when it's brash, which seems a more honest variety of the business. I realise that using the words 'honest' and 'advertising' in the same sentence is oxymoronic. One of the many advantages of being unable to operate a car is that I am able to pay more attention to my surroundings than a driver, who has to concentrate on, well, not crashing. So I'm in the car with my notebook, and for something to do I'm writing down what all these signs and advertisements have to say. I'm filling pages and pages. And then I realise something else. They're only using a very few colours, and the colours are bold, brash, and used in very visually compelling combinations. About ninety per cent of the messages that flick past my retinas are using seven colours. I start noting these down, and it's astonishing.* Red, green, blue, yellow, orange, black *and* white. *All made of plastic, all made from pigments derived from the petrochemical industry, the same hydrocarbon trade that has made the city of Los Angeles possible, at least in the short term...*

So I'm on Melrose Avenue in the Art Store,

looking for acrylic (i.e., plastic) polymer paint in red, green, blue, yellow, orange, black and white. I'm going to paint using these colours, straight from the tub. Okay. Red; cadmium red medium hue. Green; light green permanent. Blue; cerulean blue chromium. Yellow; cadmium yellow medium. Orange; cadmium orange. Any old black and white will do, as long as they're opaque.

I start painting in Los Angeles, and continue when I get back to England. It's autumn now, and I'm working in a barn in the Oxfordshire countryside. I end up spending my entire autumn and most of the winter in this barn, painting with these seven colours, painting words onto canvases that are a metre and a half square.

Part of what I'm trying to do is TREAT THE CANVAS AS 'REAL ESTATE'; I map out a district of a city and then infill with coloured blocks and words. I start with the Pacific coast, and then map the inland areas of Los Angeles. Back in the

Oxfordshire countryside L.A. *seems rather distant, and in a sort of homage to* The War On Terror *I start finding maps of other cities on the internet:* Grozny, Kabul, London, Baghdad...

I'm finding it all quite intense. I have to force myself to remember to breathe, and the repetitive aspect of using only seven colours is affecting everything I see. TREE = GREEN. HOUSE = RED. SKY = BLUE. Or BLACK. Or green. Christmas is fast approaching, and it's getting very cold in the barn, which makes holding the brush increasingly difficult, especially for painting in the words. Heroically I abandon the barn and travel to a debauched party in London. When I return the next afternoon, clutching my head, I look around at the paintings and realise that I'd finished anyway.

Haunted wall. (2003) 100cm x 100cm. Acrylic on canvas.

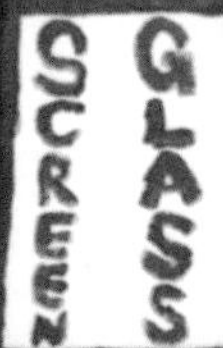

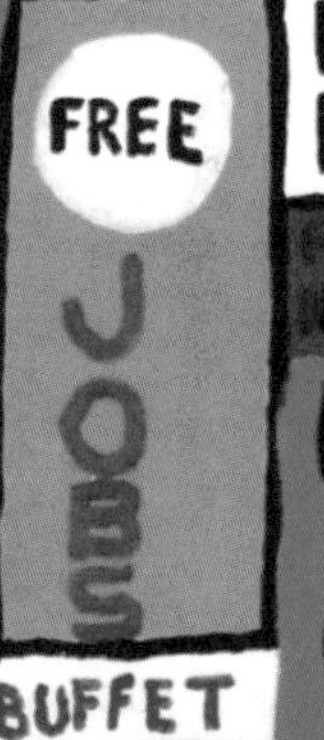

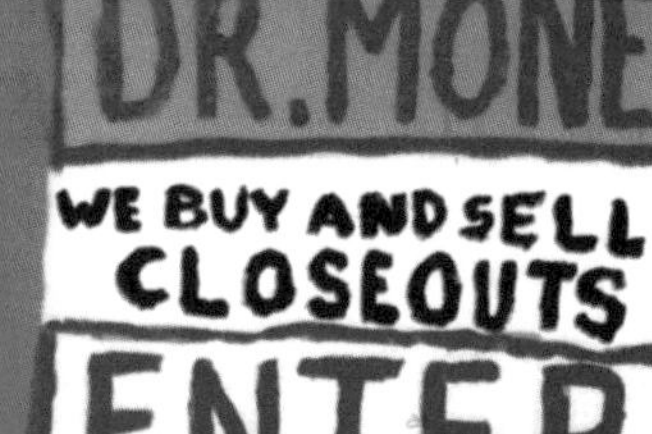

Special sauce. (2003) 100cm x 100cm. Acrylic on canvas.

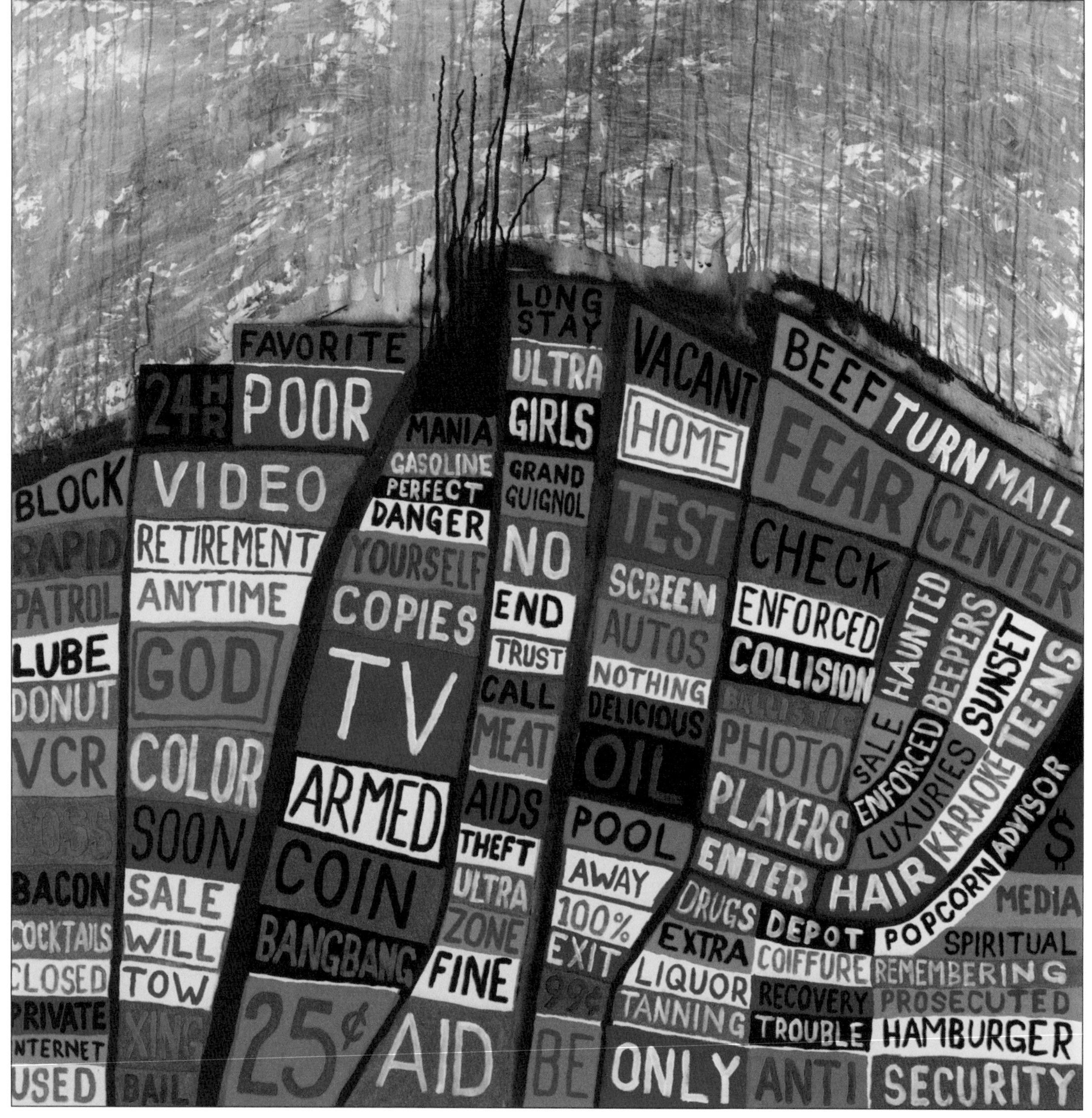

Pacific coast. (2003) 150cm x 150cm. Acrylic and blackboard paint on canvas.

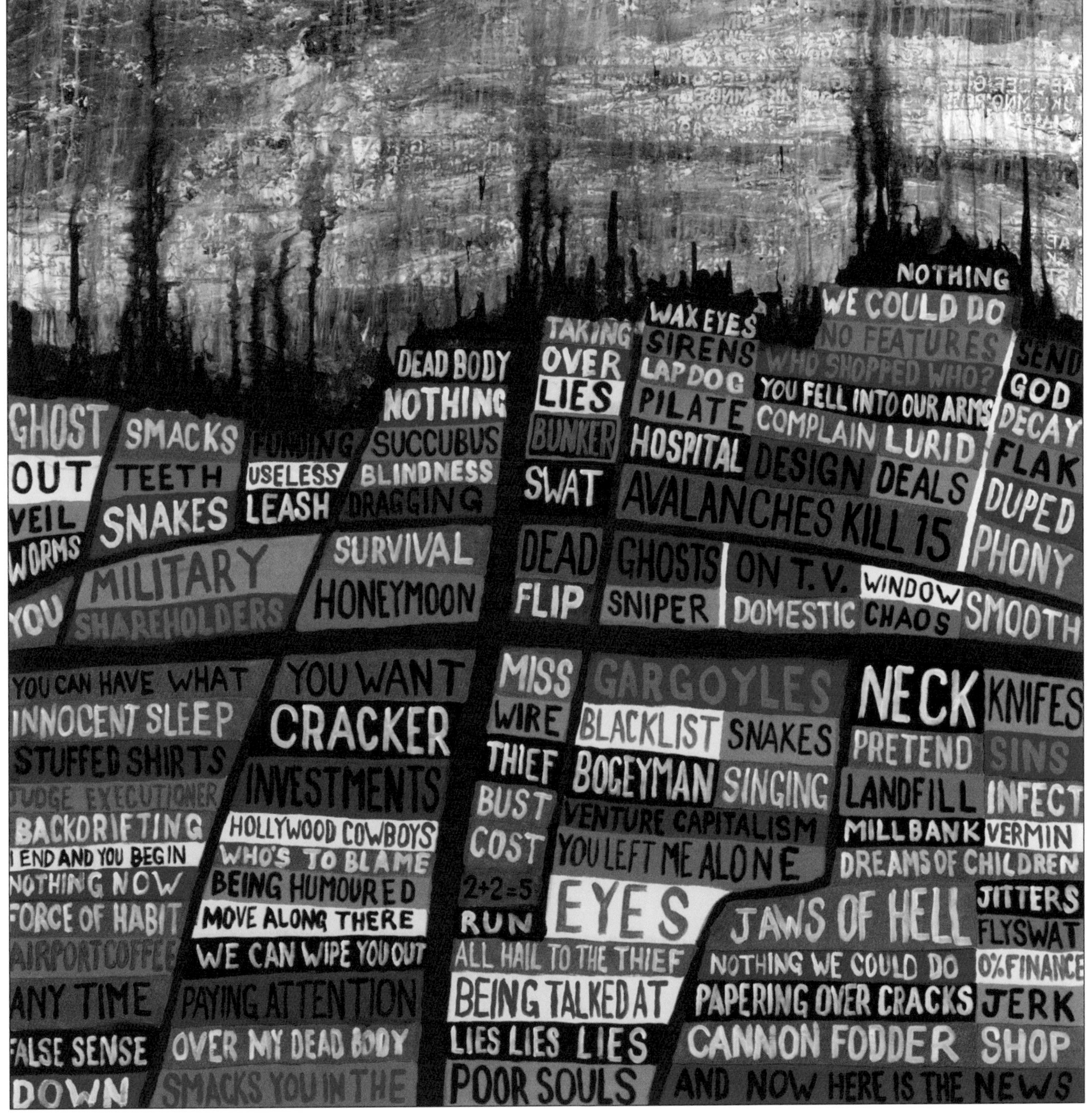

Santa Monica. (2003) 150cm x 150cm. Acrylic and blackboard paint on canvas.

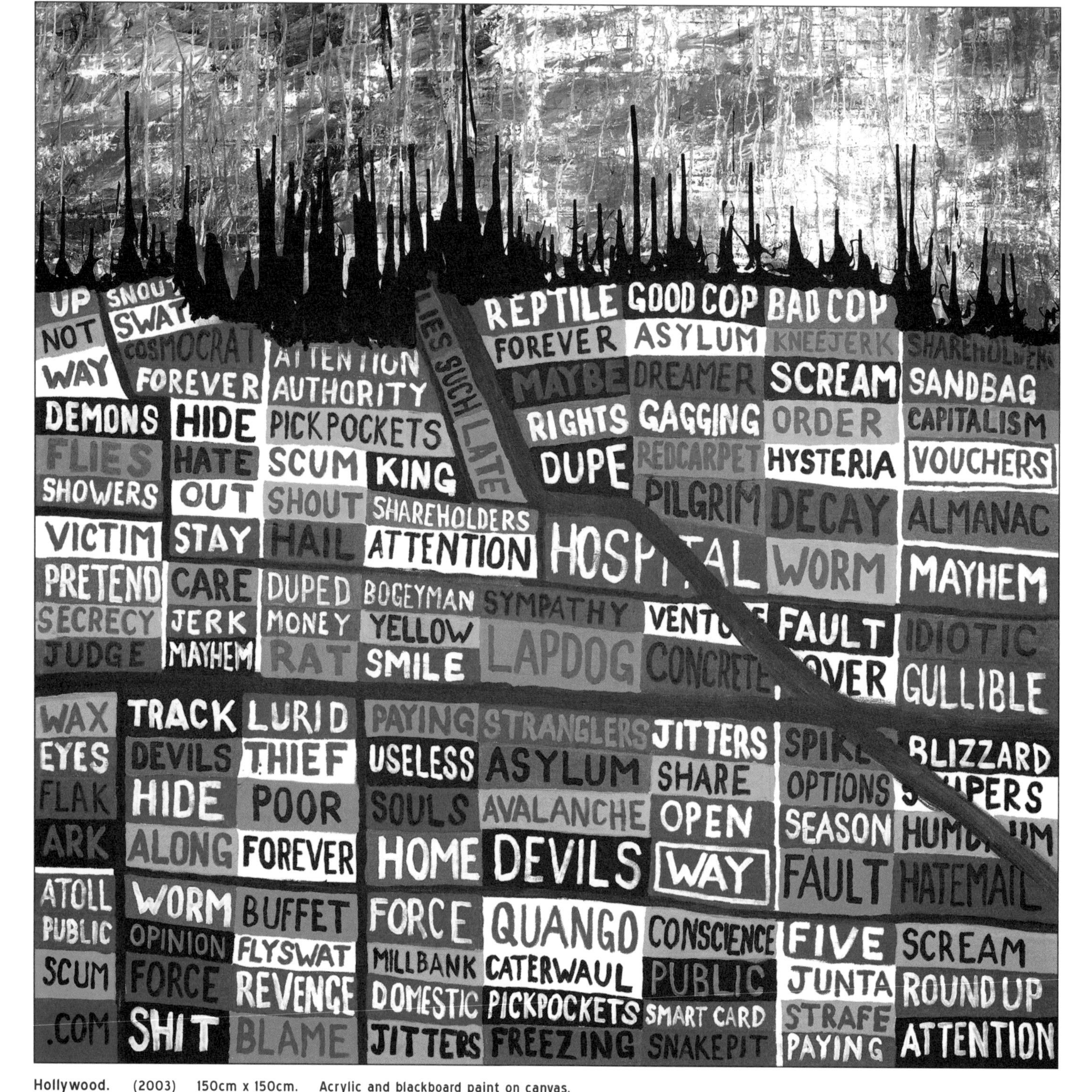

Hollywood. (2003) 150cm x 150cm. Acrylic and blackboard paint on canvas.

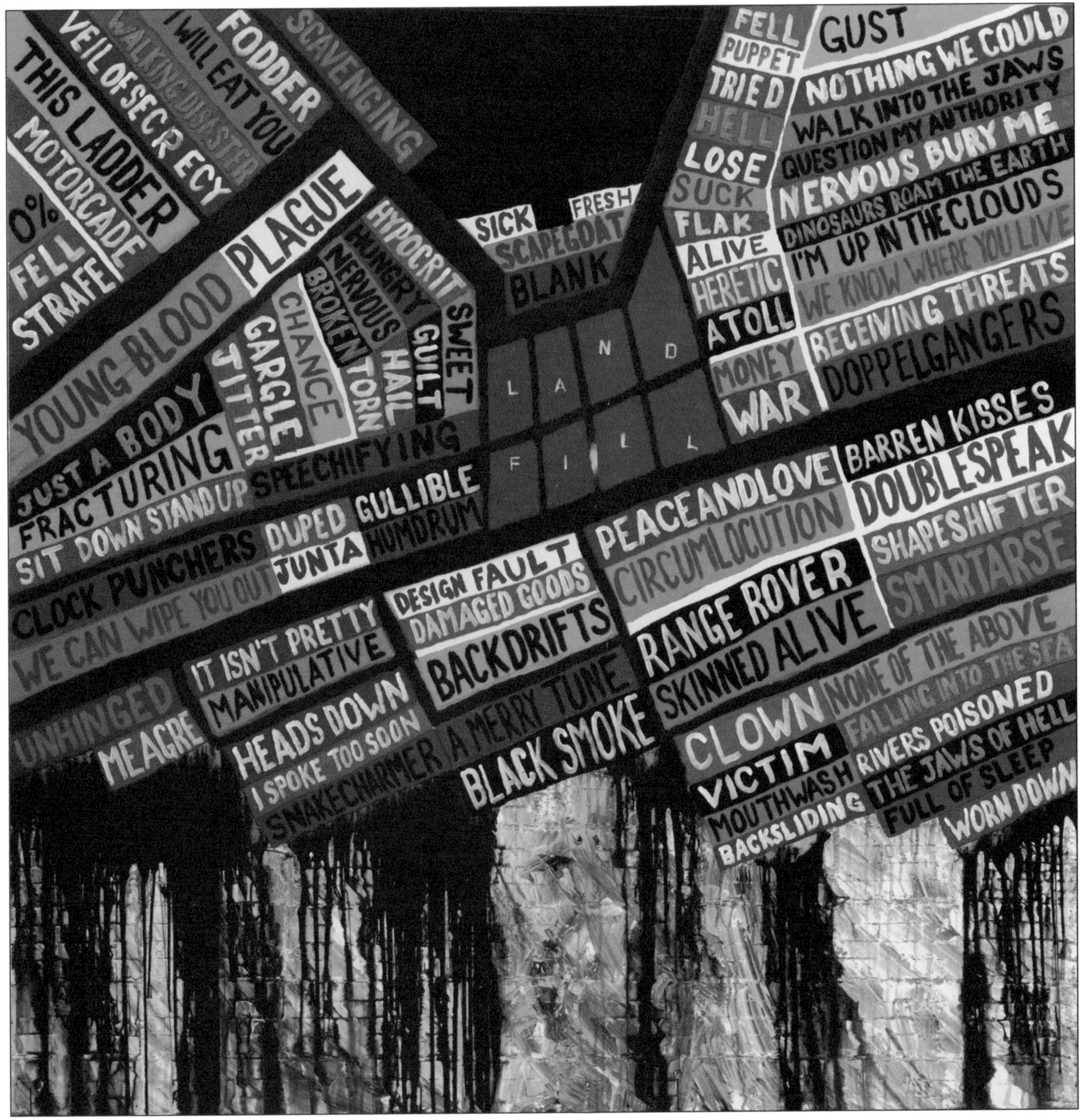

Grozny. (2003) 150cm x 150cm. Acrylic and blackboard paint on canvas.

Kabul. (2003) 150cm x 150cm. Acrylic and blackboard paint on canvas.

Baghdad. (2003) 150cm x 150cm. Acrylic and blackboard paint on canvas.

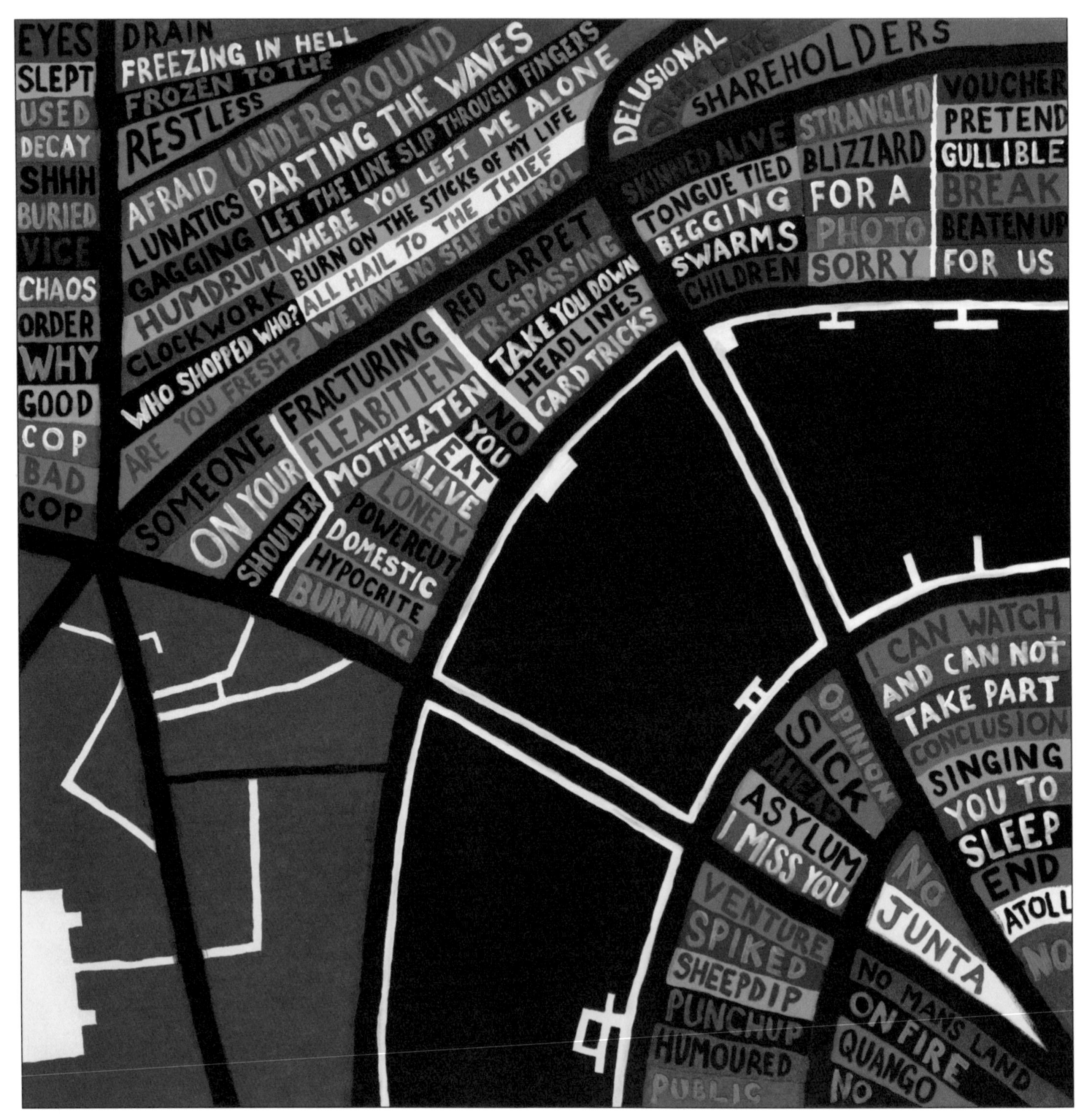

London. (2003) 150cm x 150cm. Acrylic and blackboard paint on canvas.

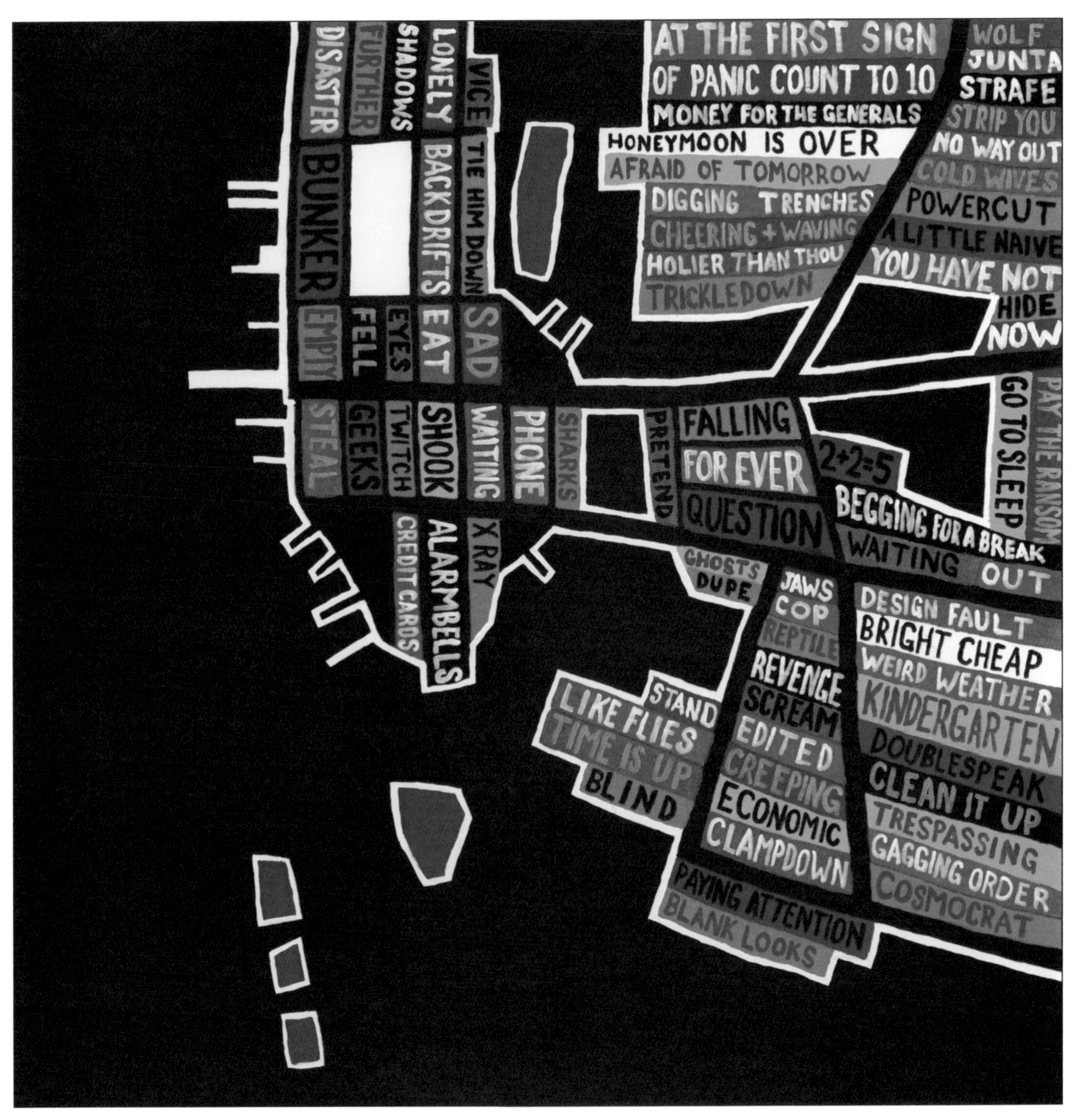

Manhattan. (2003) 150cm x 150cm. Acrylic and blackboard paint on canvas.

United states. (2004) 150cm x 150cm. Acrylic on canvas.

Hole. (2005) 150cm x 150cm. Acrylic on canvas.

NOTHING TO FEAR. NOTHING TO DOUBT.
[BEAST WITH SEVEN HEADS]
~~YOU WERE WARNED. WE KNOW~~
FRIENDS ROMANS COUNTRYMEN
WE KNOW WHERE YOU LIVE

strange all the birds.
to stake,
keep his body
for science.
Come inside this wasteland
Come and pull it apart pull me in
OWL.
OWL.
OWL.
it had a voice.
tell them how we feel whispered
creaking whispering
name children's
dead brown leaves the leaves cling on me

Kozo Cnut. (2006) 48cm x 42cm. Lino print on Japanese paper.

I am bad. I am to blame.

I think a little more sucking-up is needed.

Food and water crisis developing.

Words on a gravestone: I waited but you never came.

What will we mean? Nothing.

General loss of interest.

He'll do something silly.

Winning. The last player left in the game is the winner.

A smile like the grim reaper.

Children go to school tied together, led by parents.

Airport closed. People coughing yellow phlegm.

Not sleeping okay. Trapped in hyperspace.

DON'T GET ANY BIG IDEAS

THEY'RE NOT

GONNA HAPPEN

FINISHED.